ARE WE COMPATIBLE?

ARE WE COMPATIBLE?

·

QUESTIONS FOR COUPLES

Jeffrey A. Hoffman, Ph.D.

**Andrews McMeel
Publishing**

Kansas City

www.andrewsmcmeel.com

Library of Congress Cataloging-in-Publication Data

Hoffman, Jeffrey A., 1955–
Are we compatible?: questions for couples/
Jeffrey A. Hoffman
p. cm.
ISBN 0–8362–5424–4
1. Mate selection. 2. Marriage.
3. Marriage compatibility tests. I. Title.
HQ801.H63 1998   97–38195
306.82—dc21   CIP

98 99 00 01 02 RDH 10 9 8 7 6 5 4 3 2 1

Design by Tanya Maiboroda

To my wife, Ziva

CONTENTS

◆

PREFACE

When I was twenty-eight years old, studying psychology at the University of North Carolina at Chapel Hill, I took my grandmother on a trip to Israel. She had wanted to go there all of her life and had planned to take a trip with my aunt, but they were never able to arrange it, so I offered to take her during my summer break. She agreed and was excited. She is the most delightful, energetic elderly woman you could ever meet—sparkling eyes, quick wit, and full of wisdom. I adored her, as did all of her grandchildren and great-grandchildren. We planned our trip. We would rent a car for a month and tour the country. I had spent several months in Israel after high school, so I was able to be her driver and tour guide.

A few months before our planned trip, a professor of Jewish history from Tel Aviv University came to Chapel Hill to give a lecture. I missed the lecture but was invited to meet him with some other students for dinner. He was surrounded by young admiring female students. He was gregarious, laughing and telling stories. I was sure that he would pick one of the young women to escort him to his hotel. But when the table emptied, the two of us were left alone together. I walked with him back to his hotel and told him about my plans to visit Israel with my grandmother. Before parting, he said that I should call him when I came to Israel and he would introduce me to one of his sisters-in-law. I promised him that I would take him up on his offer.

Around that same time, I was attending a Saturday morning Bible study group with a brilliant and scholarly rabbi. One morning he gave a lecture on marriage. He told the Bible story of when Abraham sent his servant Eliezer to find a wife for his son, Isaac. Abraham told Eliezer that God would send an angel to help him find her. When Eliezer came to a well in a city, he prayed to God to send a woman who would offer water for him and his camels to drink. This would be for him a sign that God had sent a woman to be the wife of Abraham's son. Rebekah then came to the well and offered him water to drink and water for his camels. Eliezer then knew that God had made his journey prosperous.

The rabbi explained in his lecture that from this story we learn one of the most important secrets to a successful marriage. "The single most important characteristic that one should seek in a marriage partner is kindness." Beauty is pleasing, but it will fade. Intelligence is stimulating, but it will not necessarily bring happiness in marriage. The one trait that is enduring and will always bring the most satisfaction and happiness in marriage is kindness to others. This story stuck in my mind.

My grandmother and I flew to Israel and began what would become a very memorable journey—watching the sunrise over the Old City of Jerusalem, drinking coffee in a little stone-walled café among Arab taxi drivers, picking up Israeli soldiers and newly arrived immigrants hitch-hiking on the road, and meeting distant relatives who asked my grandmother why she did not try harder to find them in Europe after the war.

Nearly three weeks into our trip, I called the professor I had met in Chapel Hill. He invited us to visit him at his home. When we arrived, we met his children and one of his sisters-in-law. The sister-in-law was very friendly and invited us to join her and her other two sisters for an outdoor concert and dinner the following night. We went to the concert, and that is where I met my future wife. She was somewhat shy and distant, but had a warm and beautiful smile. Shortly after we were introduced, I offended her by asking too many personal questions. (Imagine that.) She ignored me the rest of the evening.

All of the sisters fell in love with my grandmother. They invited us to stay with them at their apartment for the remainder of our trip. We agreed. For the next week, we were treated to the hospitality and warmth of the professor's sisters-in-law. Every day they would take my grandmother shopping, exploring, and sightseeing. In the evenings after my grandmother went to sleep, we went out to the cafés along the Mediterranean. I found myself growing increasingly interested in and attracted to the middle sister, Ziva. What attracted me most was the unusual kindness she showed to my grandmother, a stranger she had known for only a few days. I remembered the rabbi's lesson and thought about the kindness shown to my grandmother, my angel.

After we returned to the States, I wrote letters to Ziva and asked her if she would consider being my girlfriend. She was polite and sincere, but after a few months she wrote to me that it was unrealistic for us to continue this correspondence. We hardly knew each other, and the distance across the ocean was too great. She said that I should get on with my life, without her. I was sad, but I accepted her request and stopped writing.

Two years later, two of Ziva's sisters, the same two we stayed with in Israel, were studying at a college in Boston. I had a new girlfriend, and while we were visiting Boston one weekend, I went alone to see the sisters. The younger sister told me that Ziva was disappointed when she heard that I had a girlfriend. I was surprised by this and could not stop thinking about it. My girlfriend at the time was pretty, intelligent, warm, and generous, but we were not really compatible. Our relationship went up and down and at times was even stormy. When we returned from Boston, we decided to spend some time apart from each other.

I wrote a letter to Ziva, asking her if there was any chance for us. Then I tore up the letter and decided to go to Israel to ask her in person. I registered for a professional conference in Israel, then called her and asked if she would have some time to spend with me during my stay. She said that she would have the time.

I will never forget the moment she answered the door to her apartment. She smiled her beautiful smile, and I wanted to hold her and never let her go. We had less than a week to spend together. I told her that I wanted to spend that time seeing if we were compatible with each other. For the next few days, we spent every hour talking and getting to know each other. We asked each other every question we could think of—about our personalities, our plans, our dreams. We talked in restaurants, walking along the beach, in the car, and until the early morning hours on her family's couch. After four days, along the shore of Lake Tiberias in the north of Israel, I asked her to marry me. I knew that it would not be easy, with both us coming from different countries and cultures. But I had a deep feeling that I had found my Rebekah. This time I was not rebuffed. Ziva accepted my proposal, and six months later we were married.

When we became engaged, we joked that one day we would write a book of questions that people could ask each other to see if they are compatible. Eleven years later, as we celebrate our eleventh anniversary, I have written this book of questions. Were we able to determine that our marriage would work by asking the questions we asked eleven years ago? Yes—I believe it helped us to see each other more clearly. Were we able to predict that we would be happy together for the rest of our lives based on our answers to these questions? No—marriage has many challenges, and success in marriage depends as much on your commitment to marriage and each other as it does on your individual personalities and compatibility. The demands of career, finances, raising children, and just surviving in today's fast-paced world put every marriage to the test—ours included.

We have found, however, that basic kindness and mutual respect are key to getting through the difficult times and finding happiness in marriage. Being compatible gives you a better start. It helped us to ask each other these questions—we hope it will help you.

INTRODUCTION

Paulo Coelho tells a beautiful story in his book *The Alchemist* about a boy searching for a treasure. On his journey, the boy meets a young woman at a well. Coelho writes:

> At that moment, it seemed to him that time stood still, and the Soul of the World surged within him. When he looked into her dark eyes, and saw that her lips were poised between a laugh and silence, he learned the most important part of the language that all the world spoke—the language that everyone on Earth was capable of understanding in their heart. It was love. Something older than humanity, more ancient than the desert. Something that exerted the same force whenever two pairs of eyes met, as had theirs here at the well. She smiled, and that was certainly an omen—the omen he had been awaiting, without even knowing he was, for all his life. What the boy felt at that moment was that he was in the presence of the only woman in his life, and that, with no need for words, she recognized the same thing.

Are We Compatible? is a book that can help you to get to know another person better and to make a thoughtful decision about your relationship with that person. It can provide a rational process for you to explore your relationship and your own feelings about that relationship.

But the union of two souls is a miraculous and mysterious process that goes well beyond my ability to comprehend or provide guidance. These questions can be used as guideposts for your thoughts, but just as important are the omens—the guideposts of your heart.

MARRIAGE

Relationships are complicated. Even under the best circumstances, maintaining a good, fulfilling relationship in marriage can be a challenge. People are inherently moody, demanding, impatient, particular, and oftentimes selfish. Sexual needs, desires, and tastes are rarely identical between two people. When you add the pressures of work, money, children, housecleaning, and living in today's complex society, it is a wonder that any marriage can survive, let alone thrive. Therefore, deciding who you will marry is possibly one of the most important decisions you will make in your life.

When you make the right decision, marriage can bring satisfaction, happiness, and moments of joy. A bad marriage can bring misery. A marriage that ends in divorce is always painful. So how do you know when you have found the right person to marry?

You are in love with this person. You cannot imagine living your life without this person. No one has ever made you feel the way this person makes you feel. No one has ever understood you or cared for you as much as this person. You could never find another person like this one. Many people base their decisions on feelings like these. But it is not enough to be in love with someone. Love alone will not sustain a couple through the ups and downs that exist in every marriage.

No marriage is going to be perfect—without any problems or conflict. When you make the commitment of marriage, you are agreeing to make compromises and accept differences. You are agreeing to work out problems together. However, it is important that you are compatible with your partner; otherwise the compromises, differences, and problems may become too great to overcome.

A friend of mine once said that marriage is 5 percent natural attraction and 95 percent work. One year after making this statement, she was divorced. Married life does require continued attention and effort. However, if you find yourself constantly having to "work" at getting along, without making much progress, then you may have some basic incompatibilities. If you have the opportunity to consider your compatibility with your partner before you get married, you should do so. You might save yourself and your partner a lot of heartache.

It is possible to become emotionally or sexually involved with someone without really knowing him or her as a person. Once an emotional attachment is formed, it may become difficult to make a rational decision about marriage. Many people allow themselves to "fall" into a relationship because of an initial attraction or temporary circumstances. They may continue the relationship because it is more comfortable, convenient, or safer to continue than to break it off. They may rationalize that the relationship is better than any alternatives they see at the time. In many cases, they become so dependent on the other person that they can no longer be objective or realistic in their thinking about the relationship.

But if you do not take control of your life and make this important decision based on your knowledge of the other person, you may be sacrificing the satisfaction that a good marriage can bring.

Compatibility is a complex phenomenon. There are many levels of compatibility. There is the level of having common interests and shared values. There is the level of compatible personal behavior, habits, and personalities. There is the level of expectations of marriage, romance, and sexual fulfillment. Finally, there is the issue of how two people communicate with and relate to each other and others outside of the marriage. Some of these aspects of compatibility are obvious and easily determined. Others are disguised by inconsistent, changing, and even contradictory thoughts and feelings each of us has about ourselves and each other.

To complicate matters even more, there are aspects of compatibility that are almost unforeseeable. These are hidden, unconscious, even dormant behaviors, and can only be glimpsed in rare moments of spontaneous actions or demeanor over time. These are the most difficult to distinguish because they are not evident by examining an individual by him- or herself, but they are manifested only in the relationship between two people. Sometimes you can even find yourself in a relationship that seems to be changing you into a different person—a person you may not like. This is not your imagination working. It may be a process I call "conscription"—when one person gets another person to follow his or her own "script."

Conscription is not a voluntary process. It is involuntary, like being drafted into service. It usually occurs when people are unconsciously seeking to repeat their childhood experience of a bad relationship with a parent. They may have felt abused, neglected, or rejected by a parent and unknowingly accepted this as their script. They may harbor a deep-seated expectation that this kind of relationship will be repeated in later intimate relationships. The surprising thing is that they often behave in ways that end up re-creating this earlier relationship. For example, a woman named Mary felt neglected by her father as a child. She married a physician, Don, who was always very busy. When he had to work long hours, Mary interpreted this as him neglecting her like her father did. She would complain to him constantly, to the point where he actually did begin to neglect her, as she always "knew" he would. She got him to follow her script. Sometimes, two people end up trying to conscript each other. That's when things get really confusing.

If you become aware of these conflicting aspects of your relationship and you do not like what you see or the way it feels, do not ignore these feelings. Explore and try to understand them, because they could be very important. If you have trouble understanding or dealing with these issues, you may want to consider talking with a professional therapist, either alone or together with your partner. The important thing is that you and your partner bring out the best in each other—not the worst.

HOW THIS BOOK CAN BE HELPFUL

How can a person possibly assess his or her compatibility with another person on all of these levels? It is difficult. There is no simple test with a compatibility score. But you can begin by asking a series of questions. Some of these questions you can discuss openly with your prospective partner. Some questions you can only ask yourself.

This book contains questions that may help you to get to know the person you want to marry. There are also vignettes of couples as examples of differences and incompatibilities between people. Your choice of a partner is a highly personal decision that cannot be based on a score or number. However, as a general guideline, if you think that you will be unhappy or dissatisfied more often than you will be happy in your relationship, then you may not be well suited for each other.

If you are already married, you should be able to answer accurately most of these questions for your spouse. Try it. You may discover positive aspects of your spouse that you were always intuitively aware of but had never verbalized. You may find that each of you have changed in fundamental ways, partly due to each other's influence, and that you would answer these questions differently today than when you were first married.

If you are unhappy with your relationship, some of the reasons for your unhappiness will most likely be revealed in the answers to these questions. The qualities that attract one person to another are often not the same qualities that ensure a good relationship. You may have become emotionally attached to someone who made you feel good and secure, especially if you were not feeling good about yourself at that time. But you may not have been compatible with that person. If this is the case, you may need to reevaluate your relationship and take a closer look at yourself and your relationship. These questions can help you to do that.

The only known predictor of whether a marriage will last or end in divorce is how they treat each other before they get married. Couples who are highly critical or negative toward each other tend to get divorced. This negativity usually arises when there are basic incompatibilities. If you find that there are many important areas in which you and your partner are not compatible, you then need to decide whether these areas of incompatibility are of critical importance to you. For instance, is this an area for which you feel so strongly that you are not willing to compromise your views or behavior—or are you willing to make compromises and accept your differences in this area?

If you find that there are important areas where there may be irreconcilable differences between the two of you, it may be best to end the relationship before it becomes too difficult for you to separate, or the relationship becomes destructive for you or other people.

If you are uncertain of what to do, you may want to seek the advice of a friend or relative, who can give you some objective feedback. You may want to go on your own, or as a couple, to speak with a counselor, minister, rabbi, or a professional therapist to help you to clarify whether or not you are best suited for each other. Some problems can be easily resolved by better communication or understanding, while other problems can be very resistant to change and may cause unending heartache. You have to use your best judgment to decide what is best for you.

This book has been designed so that, if you choose, you and your partner can write your answers or responses in the book. This will allow you to see how your perceptions and feelings change over time. It may also be interesting to look back at your responses five, ten, or even twenty-five years from now. Share them with your children and grandchildren. You may also find that by writing down your answers, certain truths about your relationship will become more evident. Whether or not you write down your answers, the most important thing is to be honest with your partner and yourself.

OPENING QUESTIONS

James and Valerie met at a party of mutual friends. There was an instant attraction and James asked Valerie to go out for coffee after the party. They talked late into the night until the waiter told them that the restaurant was closing. This was the first of many late nights of talking, going to movies, dancing, and doing other things together. In the excitement of a new romance, James neglected his normal schedule and stayed up much later at night than was his routine. He liked to go to bed early, and get up early in the morning. Valerie turned out to be a night owl, enjoying staying up late and sleeping in as late as possible.

After a year of dating, James and Valerie were so much in love that they decided to get married. They got along very well and loved to be together. However, over time, James fell back into his preferred routine of going to bed early and Valerie would stay up reading or watching TV. James would try to get Valerie to come to bed earlier, but she simply was not tired and did not want to disturb his sleep. James had other reasons for wanting Valerie to come to bed earlier but could not seem to persuade her. This led to some tension and frustration for James.

Valerie could see that their different sleep patterns was leading to a problem. She decided to come to bed earlier at least once a week. James decided to stay up late on

Saturday nights. He still got up early on Sunday morning, but he didn't mind feeling a little bit tired.

. . .

These are warm-up questions. They are simple and easy to answer, yet they begin to tell you some meaningful things about each other. Differences in these areas are not necessarily significant, and are sometimes preferable.

What is your earliest
childhood memory?
Other than your parents,
who had the most
important influence
on you growing up,
and in what way?

Q

What time of the day

are you at your best?

At that time of the day,

what are you best at doing?

What kind of music do you like? If you could spend one evening with any singer or musician in history, who would it be? Is there any kind of music that you hate?

Q

Do you have any favorite games? Are there any games that you do not like to play? What was your favorite game as a child? Can you describe a memory of yourself as a child playing one of your favorite games?

What are your favorite
kinds of movies or
television programs?
If you could become
any character from any
movie for one day,
who would it be?
Who are your favorite
actors and actresses?

INTERESTS

Jack and Hilary met at work. They both worked in management positions at the same company. They were attracted to each other and found that they shared common values. They became involved, and the passion was ignited. After dating for a while, Jack wanted Hilary to go on a camping trip with him. He was an outdoors person. He loved to hike, bike, fish, camp, canoe, and travel. Hilary did not enjoy these things. In fact, she only liked to travel if she could stay in a luxury hotel and eat at fine restaurants. Jack finally convinced her to go on a weekend sailboat trip, but Hilary was miserable. Jack told Hilary that the outdoors was a big part of his life. Hilary told Jack that she wanted to spend her free time indoors and that he would have to spend his time outdoors by himself. It turned out that Jack and Hilary had other differences, too. After the passion began to wear off, Jack decided that he would have more fun with someone who liked the outdoors. Hilary decided that she had better find someone who earned more money than Jack.

. . .

Now you are beginning to deal with questions that have more depth and significance. No two people are going to have exactly the same interests. Sometimes having different interests can bring excitement and variety to a relationship. However, having some common interests is also very important. Your interests will determine how you will spend your time together, as well as how much time you spend together. Interests are things that you enjoy doing. It is critical that you have some things that you enjoy doing together. It is also important to know how comfortable each of you will be to pursue your own separate interests that might take you in different directions.

What places would you like

to see in your lifetime?

What place in the world seems

the most romantic to you?

Where would you most

like to live?

What kinds of things
do you most enjoy reading?
What is the best book
you have ever read?
What was it about that book
that was meaningful to you?
Where and when do you
most like to read?

If you could learn any
new subject or skill,
what would it be?
Do you think you ever will
learn this subject or skill?
If so, how will you
accomplish this?

Do you like to dance?
What is your favorite
type of dancing?
How often would you like
to go out dancing?
How do you feel about
your partner dancing
with someone else?

*What are your favorite
hobbies or sports?
How much time would you
like to spend doing these
hobbies or sports?
What would you do
if you didn't have time
to do them?*

What kinds of places
do you like to go out to?
Do you prefer going out
with a group of people, or
with just one other person?
Are there any types of places
or events that you prefer
to avoid?

What do you like to do

on a rainy day when you

have no prior plans?

Do you like spending

a lot of time outdoors?

What kinds of outdoor

activities do you like to do?

WORK AND HOME

———————————————————•———————————————————

Julie had a job as a sales representative for a furniture manufacturer. Bill was a computer programmer. They had met in college and moved to Bill's hometown. Bill was close to his family, and most of Bill and Julie's friends had been Bill's friends in high school. One day, Julie was offered a promotion to the position of district manager, but it was in another city, several hundred miles away. Julie was very ambitious and had worked hard to advance in her career. They didn't have children, and Bill could easily get another job in this other city.

Bill supported Julie in her career goals, but he didn't want to leave his hometown. His parents were getting older and they relied on him more and more. Julie was afraid that she would never have this career opportunity again. Bill thought that Julie was being unreasonable and that other opportunities would become available in the city they lived in. Tension mounted, accusations ensued; it seemed that their positions were irreconcilable. Finally, Bill decided to give in to Julie's wishes. He decided that his marriage and Julie's happiness were more important to him than staying in his hometown. They moved. They visited Bill's parents as frequently as they could and eventually made new friends.

• • •

Although there are only a few questions on this topic, it is very important that you accept each other's feelings about work and home. Ambivalence about your partner's answers to these questions can lead to trouble down the road. The critical point here is not whether you agree or disagree on these issues, but rather whether you will be comfortable with each other's basic orientation to work and home. These questions also begin to reveal each other's perceptions about each of your roles in marriage as they pertain to work and home.

*How do you feel about
your work or career?
If you had the chance to
have another job or career,
what would it be?
How would you describe
your work habits?
How do you think your
peers at work see you?*

Are you the type of person who would prefer to own your own business or to have a good job? What are your work plans for the future? If you were to start your own business, what would it be?

How would you describe

your ideal home?

Which are your favorite
household chores?
Which are your least favorite?
What chores are you
willing to do?

FAMILY

David and Sandra met at a party of a mutual friend. They were attracted to each other from the moment they saw each other. From that day on they spent every day together for a year, until they decided to get married. They seemed to each other to be compatible in almost every way. They got along well with each other and enjoyed being together. They had similar backgrounds and interests. They loved each other. They wanted to spend the rest of their lives together and have a family.

It never occurred to David that Sandra might have difficulty getting pregnant. They made love often, without luck. They went to the doctor for infertility testing and found that Sandra was unable to become pregnant. Sandra longed to have a child. After a painful struggle, she accepted that she could not have her own child and she decided that she wanted to adopt a baby. David wanted a child of his own, but he was not willing to adopt a baby. He could not imagine feeling the same love and commitment to an adopted child as to one of his own.

As the years went by Sandra became more involved in her career, but David knew that she wasn't really happy. He suggested that they become foster parents, and Sandra agreed. He found himself becoming easily attached to the foster children that came into their home, and eventually they adopted a foster child whose parents had passed away. They loved the child as their own and had a fulfilling family life and marriage.

. . .

None of the following questions should be taken lightly. Before you start seriously thinking about marriage, you should have a very clear understanding of what kind of family life you want to have and what kind of interaction you want to have with each other's family. These are the kinds of issues that can make or break a marriage. If you strongly disagree on any of these questions, you should explore your feelings in depth and determine whether you could reach compromises that you could both live with, happily.

Would you like to have children? If so, at what age or time in your marriage? How many children do you want? What kinds of names would you give them?

Q

How would you deal with
a rebellious child?
What discipline techniques
would you use?
Do you believe in
spanking a child as a
means of discipline?

*What would you do if you
found out that you could not
have children naturally?
Would you want to
adopt children?
How would you react if you
adopted a child who later
wanted to meet his or her
biological parents?*

Do you enjoy spending time
with your own family?
How much time would you
like to spend with your family
on a regular basis?
How much time would you
want to spend with your
partner's family?

*What would you do if one
of your parents or close
relatives became disabled and
wanted to live with you?
What about a member of
your partner's family?
What would you do if this
disabled relative who was
living with you began to have
a negative influence on
your marriage?*

Q

*What do you think are
the most important things
that parents must do in
raising children?*

*Do you want to raise your
children according to any
specific religious practices?*

*What traits or behaviors
would bother you if your child
began to exhibit them?*

*Would you be a firm
disciplinarian with your
own children? Would you be
lenient and let them learn
from their own experiences?
If your daughter wanted to
begin having sex at an early
age without being married,
would you try to stop her,
encourage her to be careful,
or ignore the situation?
What about with a son?*

*What things did you
like about the way your
parents raised you?
What things did you not like?
What would you do or not
do like your parents?*

Q

PERSONAL VALUES

———————————◆———————————

Kathy and Ned met in college. Both were raised in fairly similar traditional religious families. Kathy rebelled against what she considered to be rigid and authoritarian rules of her family's religious practices, and she also had doubts about her own faith in God. Ned, on the other hand, accepted his family's religious practices and although during college he didn't participate in religious activities, he assumed that he would follow the traditional practices of his parents once he had a family of his own.

Kathy and Ned never really discussed this issue during their intense romance and engagement in college. They married shortly after graduation. They had a few minor disagreements over religious aspects of their wedding ceremony, but no major problems arose. A few years later, they had their first child, and then the big arguments began. They had never considered the major role that religion would play when it came to raising children. Kathy had assumed that Ned would not care much about these traditional religious customs, since in college he didn't even attend services. Ned simply assumed that once they had children, Kathy would want to raise the children the way she was raised.

The arguments continued over the years. Ned reminded Kathy of her father and of the resentment she felt when he tried to force her to participate in activities she didn't believe in. Ned and Kathy were basically compatible in most other areas, but this was a painful source of conflict over the years. If they had talked about this and reached some level of understanding with each other before they got married, they may have experienced less conflict and resentment later on.

. . .

It is important for the stability of a relationship that two people share some common values. But the most important thing is that each person has respect for the values of the other. When you are asking these questions, think about whether you genuinely respect the answers your partner gives. Think about whether you want to share your life for many years to come with a person who has these values. It is possible that some of these values will change over time as a result of maturity or even from each other's influence. However, if you do not respect your partner's basic values now, it is more likely that this will become a source of growing dissatisfaction in your relationship over time. You should also be clear about any values that you are unwilling to compromise.

What are your feelings about religion and spirituality? How do you want to practice religion in your life? How important is it that your spouse participate with you?

What values are most

important to you?

What values would you

like to place more emphasis

on in your life?

What standard of living
or material things would
you like to have?
What sacrifices would you
be willing or unwilling to
make in order to become
very wealthy?

If you had great wealth, how would you choose to spend your money and your time?

Q

What prejudices do you

have about other people?

How do these prejudices

influence the way you act?

*What are the three things
that bother you the most in
the world today?
What do you think should be
done about these things?*

Q

Do you believe in God?

What is your image or

concept of God?

Do you have any
strong political views?
Are there any political
positions you have that you
could never compromise?

What are your main

goals in life?

What about for the

next five years?

PERSONAL BEHAVIOR

Richard liked to drink beer. His father drank beer and his grandfather drank beer. He liked to have two or three beers every night after dinner. He usually didn't drink to get drunk, although occasionally at parties or on weekends he would drink to the point of drunkenness and would become loud and aggressive. When he was dating Janice, she would sometimes complain about his drinking, which Richard didn't like, but he could usually make a joke about it and laugh it off. He definitely didn't think he had a problem with alcohol and he resented any implication that he did.

Janice figured that once they got married she would be able to get Richard to stop drinking. She was wrong. The more she criticized and cajoled Richard, the more he would drink. He claimed that he could stop at any time if he chose to, but that he didn't want to stop—he enjoyed drinking. Janice became more and more worried about his drinking and began to see changes in his behavior for the worse.

One night after Richard drank six bottles of beer, Janice confronted Richard about his drinking problem. He became furious, stormed out of the house, and didn't return until early the next morning. He later apologized for his behavior, but this was just the beginning of a pattern that would repeat itself for the following several months. Janice finally gave him an ultimatum to either get treatment or get a divorce. He said that he would get help, but he never followed through. Several months later, they were separated.

· · ·

These questions are about each of your personal habits and lifestyle. Life tends to be easier for people with similar behaviors; differences can be the cause of great irritation. These are the areas of life that many married couples fight over daily, but that usually do not cause a major disruption in the marriage. If you have differences in these areas, it is best to work out some practical solutions regarding these differences before they become big problems. You may be able to prevent a great deal of daily stress in the future. However, there is an important exception to this advice. If any one of these behaviors is carried to an extreme, it can destroy a relationship, especially if it is an addiction of some sort. If this is the case, be very realistic about the situation and consult with a professional counselor if you have continuing doubts or concerns.

Do you see yourself as someone who has good manners? What manners or social behaviors would bother you in a spouse?

What are your favorite foods?

What are your least favorite?

Do you have any unusual

eating habits?

What are your sleeping habits? What would bother you the most if you were trying to go to sleep at night?

Q

*How are you at sharing a
bathroom with someone?
What things do you do in
the bathroom that might
irritate other people?
What bothers you in
the bathroom?*

Do you like going to parties where there are many people you don't know? Do you meet new people easily?

*Do you like to drink alcohol
or use any drugs?
How much do you drink
alcohol or use drugs on
a regular basis?
How do you react when you
drink alcohol or use drugs?*

Do you like to exercise?
Do you exercise on a
regular basis?
Do you prefer to exercise
alone or with others?

Are you a very neat and clean person? If you are, can you tolerate a little sloppiness? If you aren't, can you tolerate a very neat and clean person?

Would you consider yourself
a generous or stingy person
with money?
Do you believe in giving
money to charity?
How much?
Do you like to gamble
with your money?

Is it important to you
to be prompt and timely?
Do you like to have
a regular routine?
What do you do when your
routine is interrupted?

Q

How are you about

spending money?

Are you organized when

it comes to taking care

of your finances?

Would you prefer to have joint

or separate checking accounts?

Who would you prefer

to manage the finances

in the family?

PERSONALITY

Matthew was a perfectionist. He insisted on having his food prepared at a certain time, the house kept spotless, and his laundry folded in a specific manner. Nancy was aware of these tendencies when she decided to marry him, but she thought that he would help her to become more organized and productive in her own life. She agreed to serve in the traditional woman's role and to try to meet his standards. Matthew also supported Nancy's career, but he frequently criticized her for getting behind in her paperwork and not keeping appointments on time.

Matthew and Nancy loved each other very much and generally accepted each other's roles in the marriage. Matthew's constant criticism would bother Nancy, but she would rationalize that it was helping her to become more efficient. Eventually, Nancy did become more organized and efficient. She was doing well in her job, keeping the house clean, and managing to keep up with the laundry, cooking, and arranging social engagements. Matthew held up his end of the bargain by paying the bills and taking extremely good care of the house, yard, and cars. The problem was, however, that as well as Nancy performed her responsibilities, it was never good enough for Matthew. He continued to criticize and complain on a daily basis.

Nancy's resentment grew until she began to fight back. She would purposely leave things around the house, not complete tasks, and tell Matthew to do more things for himself. This led to terrible arguments. They stopped having sex and became more and more isolated from each other. Not wanting to get divorced, Nancy suggested that they see a marital therapist, and Matthew agreed. In therapy they learned to make more compromises, redistribute the household tasks, and be less critical of each other. Their love was rekindled, they resumed sexual relations, and their marriage was strengthened.

. . .

Personality is at the heart of compatibility. Your personality reflects the way you look at the world, how you feel about yourself, and how you feel about others. Your personality may change in some aspects over time, but in most respects it will remain relatively constant. It is sometimes difficult to describe your own personality, and others may see you differently than you see yourself. Nevertheless, if you and your partner can answer the following questions honestly, you can get a pretty good sense of each other's basic personality traits. There are no right or wrong answers. The critical task here is to be as honest and objective with your partner and yourself as possible to determine whether you feel that you will be compatible with each other.

It is often said in regard to personality characteristics that "opposites attract." This may be true to some extent, and for some couples it might provide stability and satisfaction if each partner has some characteristics that complement the other. However, there is also a danger in seeking characteristics in someone that are the opposite of your own. For many couples, opposite characteristics that were an initial attraction in their relationship can become the same characteristics that they cannot tolerate some years later in their relationship.

This seems to be especially true when you are attracted to a characteristic in your partner that you feel is missing or lacking in yourself. For instance, you may be painfully shy and your partner very outgoing. Initially, you complement each other, the outgoing partner helping the shy partner to open up and the shy partner bringing a calmness to the relationship. As you mature and grow, even as an adult, you may become more confident in yourself, and choose to express yourself more openly. Your partner may begin to feel that you no longer need him or her for some of the basic qualities that initially attracted you to him or her. You may also come to resent this quality in your partner if you perceive that he or she is stifling your growth in this area.

As you discuss these questions, make sure that you look deeply enough into yourself and your partner to determine whether the characteristics that you value in your partner now are likely to be the same qualities you will value over the years to come. In a good relationship you may feel that your partner "completes" you, which can bring a feeling of ultimate satisfaction. Just be careful that you truly value the qualities in your partner that make you feel complete, and that you are not using your partner to resolve something within you that you eventually may work out yourself.

What are your best qualities?

What are your worst

characteristics?

Do you think of yourself as a realist or are you more of an idealist or dreamer? How do other people see you? What things are you more realistic about and what things do you dream about?

Are you the kind of person who

likes to take risks in life or do

you prefer to take a more slow

and sure approach to things?

What are some examples?

Are you a jealous person?

What makes you jealous?

How do you react when

you get jealous?

What makes you angry? What do you do when you get angry? What do you do when you really lose your temper? How do you like others to respond to you when you are angry? How long does it usually take you to get over your anger?

Q

Do you consider yourself a shy, inhibited, or introverted person, or are you more outgoing and extroverted? In what situations are you most and least comfortable?

Do you consider yourself a person whose mood changes frequently, or does your mood generally remain the same? What things influence your mood?

*How do you act
when you get sick?
How do you like other
people to treat you when
you are sick?*

Q

What makes you happy?

What makes you laugh?

What makes you feel good?

Do you consider yourself a high-energy person, low-key, or fairly even-keeled? Are you an active "doing"-type person or a passive "being"-type person? How do you feel about being with someone who has very high or low energy?

Are you generally more tense

or more relaxed?

How do you handle stress?

What kinds of things

cause you stress?

What are your greatest

fears in life?

If you are working on a project
and run into one obstacle
after another, would you
rather keep working on it or
go on to something else?
What is the most frustrating
task you have faced
in your life?

Do you like to keep things
organized, or do you generally
let things go until you have
to deal with them?
What kinds of things do
you tend to let go?

What would you do
if you became disabled?
How would you handle it?

What would you most like
to change in yourself?
What would you most like to
change in your partner?

RELATING TO OTHERS

Tom was a very good-looking man. Judy was also very physically attractive, but she didn't think of herself as being as attractive as others found her to be. Wherever Tom went, women would notice him and frequently women would flirt with him. Judy knew that she could basically trust Tom, but he had a very friendly and outgoing personality, and women would sometimes think that he was flirting with them as well. This would drive Judy crazy, and she would become extremely jealous when other women started to flirt with Tom.

Judy tried to convince Tom not to be so outwardly friendly to other women. She told him that he was sending them the wrong signals. But he couldn't see it. He felt like he was just being himself and that she had nothing to worry about. Judy would try to overcome her feelings of jealousy, but then they would suddenly rise up within her and completely take over her emotional state. Tom began to resent Judy's apparent lack of trust in him and would accuse her of driving him to the point of wanting to have an affair, which of course made Judy feel even more jealous and insecure.

Then one day Judy answered the telephone and a woman asked for Tom. Judy asked who it was and the woman hung up the phone. Judy was convinced that Tom was having an affair. She went into a panic and accused him of lying to her. He was lying. Tom did have an affair and eventually he admitted it. After a tremendous amount of pain and suffering, they got divorced.

• • •

These questions regarding the way you relate to others reflect another dimension of your personality, maybe the most important in marriage. These questions reveal whether you will treat your spouse, your friends, and your children with respect. It may be difficult for your partner to answer some of these questions honestly, especially if he or she might be taking the chance that you may look at him or her in a more negative light. So you must listen carefully to the answers and try to assess whether the answers are consistent with the way that your partner really interacts with you and others. Personality characteristics and behavior patterns are very difficult to change. So you must be sure that you feel compatible with your partner in the way he or she relates to you and others.

What is the hardest thing

for you to accept or tolerate

in another person?

How do you deal with it?

How do you feel about

sharing personal belongings

with someone else?

Are there any things that you

would rather not share?

Do you tend to be stubborn
about your views and opinions
or are you flexible and open
about changing them?
What views are you most
stubborn or inflexible about?

Are you open to taking criticism or do you tend to be sensitive or defensive when someone criticizes you? What kinds of things do you tend to criticize in others?

Are you a person who usually

gets what you want,

or do you usually give in

to the wishes of others?

What things do you

insist on getting?

*Do you consider yourself
an affectionate person?
Do you like to receive
a lot of physical affection?
How do you feel about
people displaying affection
in front of others?*

Do you consider yourself
a talkative person?
Is it difficult for you to
share your feelings with
another person?
What kinds of things do you
most like to talk about?

*Is it important to you to
have frequent intellectual
conversations with your mate,
or are you content to talk about
ordinary everyday events
and matters?*

Do you consider yourself
a forgiving person?
For what things would you
be willing to forgive
another person?
For what things could you
never forgive someone?

What gives you confidence

and trust in another person?

In what ways are you

trustworthy?

Do you trust people readily

or do people have to earn

your trust over time?

What would it take for

someone to break your

trust in them?

Do you like to share in
making decisions, prefer to
make most decisions yourself,
or have someone else
make the decisions?
What things do you prefer
to decide yourself?

Q

*Are you readily willing
to admit when you have
made a mistake or
do you tend to deny it?
Are you able to laugh at your
own mistakes or misfortunes?
What have been some of your
biggest mistakes in life?*

COMMUNICATION

⎯⎯⎯⎯⎯⎯⎯⎯⎯⎯⎯⎯ ◆ ⎯⎯⎯⎯⎯⎯⎯⎯⎯⎯⎯⎯

Sam and Fran had a very stormy premarital relationship, with periods of intense passion and love, divided by periods of intense fighting and tension. During one particularly romantic period, they got married. Not surprisingly, the previous pattern continued into their marriage. Their friends thought that they were perfect for each other because they were both full of life and energy, while being strong-willed and quick-tempered at the same time.

A few years later, Sam played on a softball team with a very attractive woman who was attracted to him, and she repeatedly invited him over to her apartment for a drink after games. Sam and Fran's marriage had reached an especially low point, as they had been fighting incessantly over money. One day, Fran went out and bought a new car, which Sam didn't think they could afford. After his next softball game, he went to the other woman's apartment, and after a couple of drinks they had sex. Afterward, Sam felt guilty about it and knew that if he told Fran she would leave him. When he returned home that night, he started a fight with Fran over the new car, and she never noticed the difference.

A few months later, the fighting subsided and the passion was rekindled. Soon they were feeling closer than ever and forgot all about their financial problems. Sam continued to feel bad about the affair and resolved never to let it happen again. He never mentioned a word about it to Fran or anyone else. He suspected that Fran may have had an affair during their months of fighting, but he never asked her about it. Sam and Fran went on to have children and a fulfilling family life. They continued to have their fights, but they remained faithful to each other from that point on.

. . .

The following questions relate to how you communicate with other people and how you express your feelings. The way you communicate may reveal some aspects of your personality, but it also reflects the way you learned to express yourself growing up in your family. People can learn new ways to communicate and express feelings that can greatly enhance the way couples relate to each other and feel about each other. Thus, in examining your compatibility with your partner it is not only important to decide how you feel about your partner's answers to the following questions, but also, how willing and able your partner is to learn to communicate in a way that would make you feel more comfortable.

What do you think is the best

way to resolve a problem

between two people?

Do you usually resolve your

problems this way?

Q

When something is bothering you, do you talk about it or hold it in?

When someone is extremely upset with you, would you prefer that she tell you immediately or wait until she calms down to discuss it with you?

*What would you do if you
found out that you had hurt
someone else's feelings?
Is it difficult for you to
apologize to someone when you
have been wrong or insensitive
about something?*

*If someone emotionally
hurts you or hurts someone
close to you, what would
you do about it?
Would you want to get back
at the person in some way?*

Q

*Do you usually let
other people know how
you feel about them?
In what ways do you
show it?*

Do you like to talk about your personal experiences from the past? How do you feel about keeping some experiences or thoughts secret from your partner?

Do you feel that couples should be completely honest with each other, or that sometimes it is better to tell a "white lie" in order to keep from hurting the other person's feelings? What kinds of things would you not want to be completely honest about?

ROMANCE, MARRIAGE, AND SEX

Joe and Gloria had a great sexual relationship early in their marriage, with intense lovemaking two or three times a week. But after having two children, and with both of them holding full-time jobs, keeping up the house, trying to keep in physical shape, and just coping with the problems of everyday life, Gloria was tired and had less energy for making love than she used to. Although Joe was also frequently tired, his desire for frequent sex did not diminish at all, and he became increasingly frustrated and angry at Gloria's unwillingness to make love more than once every couple of weeks.

Joe tried to woo Gloria with fancy dinners out and by bringing home gifts and roses, but it always seemed that there was something else that had to be done in the house or the children were sick or something else that kept Gloria from having the time or mood for making love. As much as Joe tried to be understanding, he felt a growing hostility because he felt that Gloria wasn't responding to his needs. Joe would complain and harass Gloria, which only made her feel less inclined to make love.

One day Joe's anger burst into a big fight with Gloria. He told her that he loved her and wanted to stay married to her, but that he didn't want to go on feeling sexually frustrated. Gloria cried in exasperation and argued that it wasn't that she loved him any less, but that she just couldn't keep up with the demands placed on her. They talked late into the night and eventually Joe offered to give up his membership at the health club so that he could spend more time helping Gloria at home. Gloria accepted his offer, felt his genuine desire to be sensitive to her needs, and invited him to make love with her. They still didn't make love two or three times a week, but it was more frequent than before, and much more satisfying.

. . .

You and your partner's views on romance, marriage, and sex are very important in deciding whether you are compatible enough with each other to get married. If each of your views and opinions appear to be very different from each other's as revealed by your answers to some of these questions, you may not be very compatible with each other for marriage. Your relationship should be able to handle some degree of differences in these areas, but you must decide for yourself how strongly you feel about your own personal views. Some of these questions can be highly sensitive and personal and may be difficult to answer. But these are important issues that you will face in any marriage and it is best to know how your partner feels about these questions before you make such a momentous commitment.

How would you describe your

ideal romantic evening?

*How important
is romance to you?
What things would
you do to keep a sense of
fun or romance in
your marriage?*

What values are most important to you in marriage?

How do you feel about individual "private time" in marriage? How much time do you like to spend alone?

*How frequently would you
want to get together with
friends as a couple?
What kinds of things do you
like to do with other friends?
If your spouse wanted to
spend some time with old
friends without you,
would you object?
What about friends of
the opposite sex?*

Q

Would you mind if your partner wanted to meet with a former boyfriend or girlfriend for a casual lunch?

If your marriage was generally satisfying but your partner had a brief affair with another person, would you prefer to be told about it or would you rather not know?

Q

What would cause you to want to get a divorce? What would you be willing to do before getting a divorce if you were unhappy with your marriage?

Q

What things in your life are of such a high priority that you cannot compromise them?

Q

What would you do if your
spouse wanted to move to
another city for a better job,
but you were happy living
where you were?

Q

*What are your views on
the role and responsibilities
of the man and the woman
in marriage?*

Q

How important is sex to you?
How often would you like to
have sex? What would
you do if your spouse became
less physically or sexually
attractive to you?

If you were having a problem

or discontentment with

your sex life, how would

you deal with it?

How would you like your

spouse to deal with a sexual

problem or discontent?

YOU AND ME

George always admired his wife Karen's kindness toward others and her sensitivity toward people less fortunate than herself. Karen admired George's ability to overcome adversity and to find something positive in every situation. They both knew of each other's respect for these qualities and would often comment on them when describing their spouse to others.

Then a tragic thing happened. Karen's sister was disabled in an automobile accident. Her sister had three young children and was now unable to walk or drive a car. Karen gave up everything to help out her sister. She quit her job, gave up her social activities, and neglected her housework in order to help her sister and take care of the children. She was also very depressed to see her sister in this condition and became preoccupied with her sister's problems. She gave less and less attention to George as a result.

This became a very difficult situation for George because while he admired Karen's devotion to her sister and he tried to maintain a positive attitude, he felt increasingly alienated and isolated from Karen. At one point he tried to discuss these feelings with Karen, but Karen reacted defensively, stating that she had no control over the situation and expressed resentment that George appeared to be criticizing her for making sacrifices for her sister. But once Karen overcame her initial defensiveness, she realized that she had been neglecting her marriage, as well as herself. She eventually decided to go back to work and to help pay for child care for her sister's children. She spent more time with George, and he was grateful for his wife's enduring quality of kindness that had first attracted him to her.

．．．

Marriage is most fulfilling when you can see your positive qualities reflected in the eyes of your spouse. A good marriage should reaffirm your basic goodness as a person. When you feel that your relationship helps you to grow as a person and to become more secure with your own sense of self, your relationship will flourish. If your relationship makes you feel bad about yourself or you feel that it changes you in ways that you do not like, then you need to either work out some problems with your relationship or within yourself, or find someone with whom you are better suited.

What is it that you like most about your partner?

What qualities do you most respect in your partner?

If you could change
one thing about your partner,
what would it be?
What other things would you
change about your partner?
How would you feel if these
things did not change?

How will you help your spouse

to grow as a person?

Q

DREAMS
AND WISHES

Alex's dream in life was to become a politician, to make a contribution to society by advocating for his beliefs in equality and justice. Monica's dream was to combine a successful private law practice with raising children. Alex and Monica met when they were in law school together. They fell in love and felt compatible with each other in many ways. They got married and both began extremely successful careers in private law practice and were becoming financially well off.

Several years later, they were both feeling the pull of their dreams. Alex wanted to enter politics, and Monica wanted to have children. The only problem was that this would mean that they would have to take a drastic cut in their income and make a major change in the lifestyle to which they had become accustomed. Alex's income as a politician would be much less than it was as a private attorney, and Monica would have to stop work for a while and then cut back on her practice for several years. Monica suggested that Alex wait several more years before entering politics, but Alex felt that if he didn't make the move soon, it would be too late for him and he would never satisfy his real desires.

Alex and Monica decided that their dreams were more important than the material quality of their lifestyle, and that each of their dreams were of equal importance. They sold their house and expensive cars and moved into a smaller townhouse. Alex was elected in his first political race. Monica gave birth to two girls in three years. They had difficult times financially, and they had the ordinary ups and downs that come with marriage and family life, but they loved and respected each other for making the sacrifices necessary so that they could both pursue their most important dreams.

. . .

Dreams and wishes are sometimes just as important as reality in keeping a relationship together. The dreams you share may be the lifeblood of your relationship. If you are compatible with each other in most aspects of your relationship, it is your dreams that will carry your relationship to higher levels of fulfillment.

*If you could go back and
change anything in your past,
what would it be?*

If you could guarantee

one thing in your future,

what would that be?

*How would you like
to see yourself and your life
ten years from now?
What about twenty-five or
even fifty years from now?*

Q

What is your greatest

dream in life?

Q

EPILOGUE

———————————◆———————————

Only with understanding, kindness, respect, and commitment can marriage weather the seasons and storms of life. Love and romance are vital and wonderful, but these are feelings that will inevitably vary in intensity over the years. They are also feelings that can change suddenly, if you discover something in your partner that you were not aware of and do not like. Or they can change gradually, if there are basic aspects of your partner that you never liked but had tried to ignore or minimize early in your relationship.

Many couples will read this book and come to the conclusion that they are absolutely not compatible with each other—and still get married. There are many reasons people stick together, some of which are hard to understand. If you marry someone with whom you have many basic incompatible ways of being, try to work it out. Get help from a counselor who is experienced in these matters, and see whether compromises or allowances can be made that will make the relationship more satisfying than destructive. For many people, being in a less-than-satisfying relationship is preferable to being alone or in desperate search of an ideal romantic relationship. Each person must make the decision that is best for him or her.

Life is short. Make your decisions wisely.

JEFFREY A. HOFFMAN, PH.D., is a clinical psychologist who specializes in marital therapy, drug treatment, and HIV prevention. He is the president of Danya International, Inc., a health and human services consulting firm based in Silver Spring, Maryland. He is married to Ziva and they have three children.